Boneyard Voice

POEMS AND PHOTOGRAPHS FROM THE EDGE OF DARKNESS

Pat O'Keefe

Reaper Publishing

Boneyard Voice

POEMS AND PHOTOGRAPHS FROM THE EDGE OF DARKNESS

Reaper Publishing

ISBN-13: 978-0692872123 (Reaper Publishing)
ISBN-10: 0692872124

Printed in the United States of America

Table of Contents

Poetry & Photography Macabre

Credits

Dedicated to
Ken O'Keefe
My husband. My love. My muse.

Ode to the Graveyard Poets

Memento Mori

The literary cemeteries of the great graveyard poets were littered with reminders of death. Skulls and crypts were the backdrop for agonizing emotions caused by loss and introspection.

Poets such as the Reverend Thomas Parnell and Thomas Gray would focus the industry of their pens on the vanity of human pretensions. Revealing how all that we create as humans will eventually rot through the decay that both death and time conspire to bring to us, personally.

The works of the graveyard poets and of those who would follow during the era of Dark Romanticism are the inspiration for **Boneyard Voice**. It is the mournful and melancholy words of Edgar Allan Poe, in particular, that have haunted my work. However, words such as these from Reverend Parnells' poem, *A Night-Piece on Death*, influenced Poe's work:

> Those Graves, with bending Osier bound,
> That nameless heave the crumbled Ground,
> Quick to the glancing Thought disclose
> Where Toil and Poverty repose.

This influential early piece of "graveyard poetry" was published posthumously by Alexander Pope in 1722.

As melodious as Parnell's poem is to the ear of one who has the understanding that vanity is futile, Thomas Gray's masterpiece, *Elegy Written in a*

Country Churchyard, is a symphony of images all relating to. . .death. In the following partial stanza, Gray focuses on the inevitability of our ultimate demise.

> Give anxious Cares & endless Wishes room
> But thro' the cool sequester'd Vale of Life
> Pursue the silent Tenour of thy Doom.

One of the best-known poems in the English language is *Elegy Written in a Country Churchyard.* But as popular as it was, graveyard poetry eventually gave way to a new way of looking at life and death. Ironic in itself, as this transition may have made proof to their mind that nothing is forever.

In America, the dark romanticists who captured the imaginations of the people included literary geniuses such as Nathaniel Hawthorne, Herman Melville, and the incomparable Edgar Allan Poe.

Like thousands of other authors since Poe wrote his great works, my writing is inspired by him. The richness of his words, the turn of the plot, the romantic and gloomy atmosphere that he created, all conspired to feed my active and hungry imagination.

Even in my photography, I can see where his dark version of the world helped me to craft my own artistic vision. In addition to his poetry, his short stories spurred me to write and to photograph the subjects and locations at which I have chosen to point my pen and camera.

But, it is the spirit of his well-thought-out verses that ring out throughout the words in this book. Written illustrations of love, loss, decay, and death, all but the first guaranteed to be felt by those on this planet we call Earth. The following stanza, the last in Poe's poem, *The Raven*, is an example of the power of his words. One can also hear the grim influence of the graveyard and its poets.

> And the Raven, never flitting, still is sitting,
> *still* is sitting
> On the pallid bust of Pallas just above my
> chamber door;
> And his eyes have all the seeming of a
> demon's that is dreaming,
> And the lamp-light o'er him streaming throws
> his shadow on the floor;
> And my soul from out that shadow that lies
> floating on the floor
> Shall be lifted—nevermore!

I am Pat Bussard O'Keefe, a photographer, poet, author, psychic medium, paranormal investigator, and dreamer. The landscape of the otherworld is one that I traverse on a regular basis. It is a place where the dead dwell and emotions take form; where there is no limit to the human potential and where metaphysical laws supersede those of the physical world. Join me there. Your ticket lies within the words of this book.

Pat O'Keefe
pat-okeefe.com
hauntedphotographer.com

Poetry Macabre

Boneyard Voice (Advice from the Dead)

When Death came for me
It was with gentle hand
That breath and life were separated.

A loss of voice in the earthly realm,
But, given more, much more in the next,
The Great Unknown.

Peace, joy, love, words disconnected
Spirit reconnected to God.
A relationship torn by the life I chose in this soul-
cycle.

If I could but whisper, from where I am, to those
who fear the Reaper of Souls...
When it is your time, go, let go, there are those
that wait for you.
Death is the catalyst for a great reunion.

And, when you cross that watery divide,
May your soul weigh lighter than the feather
held by Anubis in the balance.

Hear my voice, faint though it may be,
There are Two Paths
One will balance, the other will not.

Choose wisely.

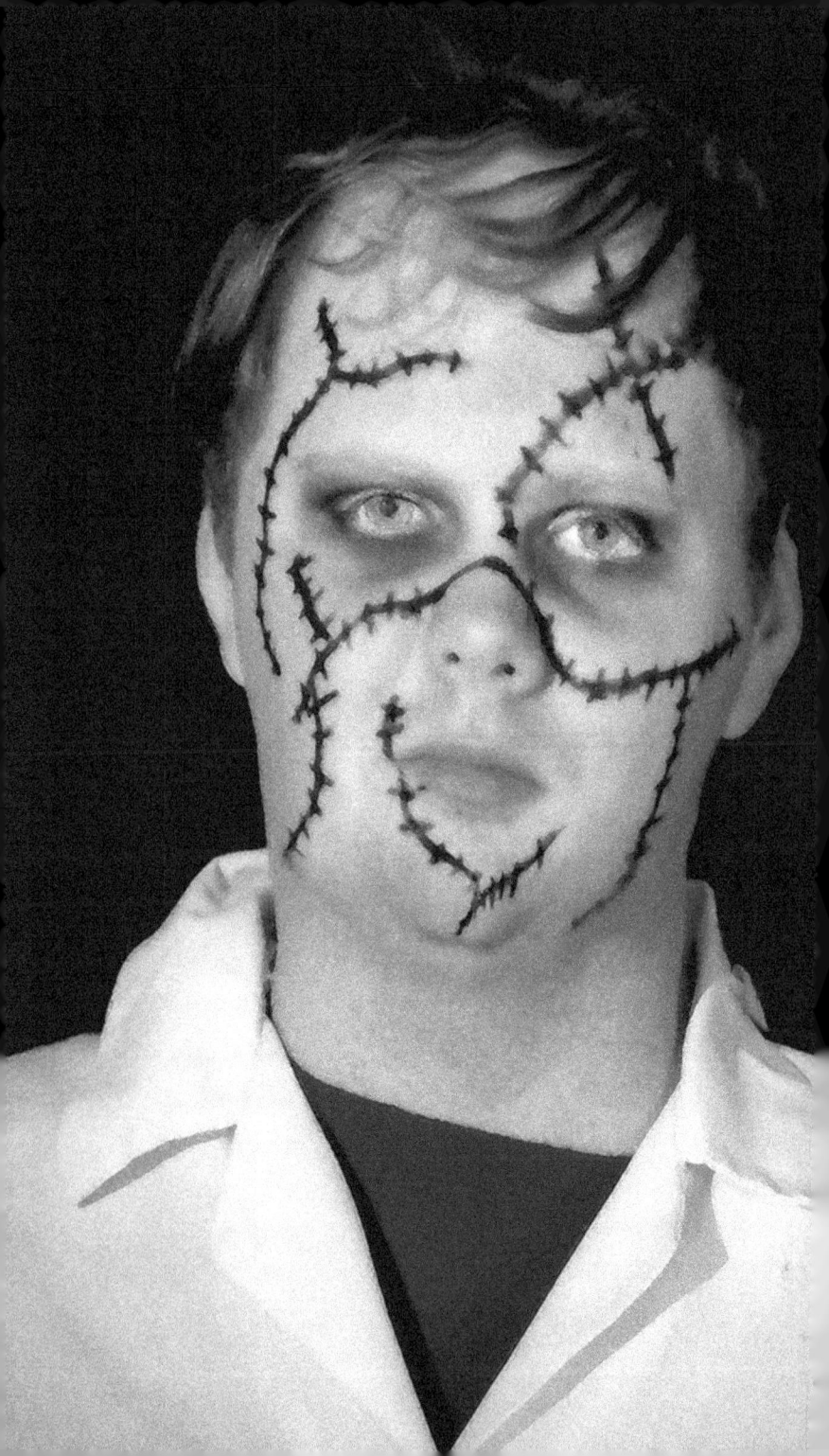

Stitches

My young mistress made me one night.
Into her nightmare world, I came.
A man, made from other men,
One criminal brain inserted.

I cannot gaze upon myself.
Others turn away from me.
"Monster," I have heard them say,
While staring at my visage.

My cursed face outlined in stitches.
All other evidence of shame is covered.
I ponder the words of the villagers,
Could my ugliness have caused their hatred?

I would gladly give all that I have.
But, owning nothing and expecting less.
To have them understand that within this
mangled form,
Beats the heart of a wounded man.

Rejected by all and loved by none.
I pine for golden sunshine.
Instead, my place is in the shadows,
Alone, afraid, forgotten.

My mistress, Mary is so fragile and lovely.
Her lover, Percy and friend, George are
handsome.
It is an irony that from such beauty,
Was born a beastly creature.

The years have passed so quickly.
My humanity still ignored.
Within my soul a battle rages,
Between the wicked mind and the heart that
yearns to soar.

Mary's beauty has long since faded.
She sleeps the longest sleep.
But I have remained with her and you,
In nightmare lands, I weep.

FEB 1855

JU 1906

Monument

In cold marble stone
memory is etched deeply
into hearts and rock.

The Watchers

Watch over me,
The dead,
As our ancestors did before,
Strewing flowers before decay,
Decorating our final pallet.
Three days
Of darkness
Dreadful.

Watch for movement
Of hand or foot,
Of face or limb,
Of blinking eye or rasp of breath,
Of beating heart or mirror's fog.
Three days
Of darkness
Dreadful.

Watch my body,
Blood washed clean,
Now, colored by Death's palette,
Mottled grays and purples,
As shadows play across gaunt features.
Three days
Of darkness
Dreadful.

Watch as others come,
Gathering of family and friends,
Of those who cared and those pretenders,
A viewing, a wake, a goodbye,
Fading light on somber faces.
Three days
Of darkness
Dreadful.

Watch over me,
The dead,
Until the peacocked hearse is gone,
Until the last spade of earth is turned,
Until you release me to the soil.
Three days
Of darkness
Dreadful.

Ruined Hospital

She stands
sentinel to echoes
of souls distressed
withering and trapped
within cold walls
eternal night prevails.

She hides
misery, loss, death
of spirits silenced
in dark hallways
rooms sunlit starved
voices quieted eternally.

She screams
in muted voice
to all comers
within her bowels
time jumps erratically
day is night.

She welcomes
all foolish visitors
and unwise are all
who enter within,
through doors, broken windows
. . .Welcome to Hell.

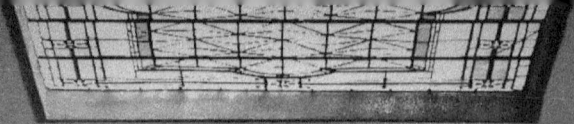

New Residence

Where once I had a grand abode
My new home, small and humble
Neighbors' silent, still, and cold
This manse, it needs no lumber.

In winter, with its killing frost
Or summer's honeysuckle sweetness
The world above, connections lost
To death, I have borne witness.

Cruel Kronos peeled the decades back
From the timeline of my life
Leaving corpse husk upon the rack
Of faded memories, like sharpened knives.

For those who would remember me
An imperfect life lived perfectly
I now lay here waiting patiently
For you and God and Eternity.

Ascension

The release of souls
Great cycle of birth and death
Reincarnation

Freedom

I see you as last we met, lovely in the spring of life
Yellow dress above the knee, my pale and lovely wife
The sun was bright, its rays did warm
Before unleashed, strong winds, a storm
I cowered with my prayers and thoughts
In a nightmare, we were caught.

I see you as last I glanced
Upon your sweet, still countenance
The sun snuffed out all warmth; now cold
Colors drained and heart once bold
Now weak and tired
In grief and pain, I am deeply mired.

I see you as I take a breath
My last, before the dance of Death
I wish to touch the other side
Where I will find my waiting bride
I ask no tears, wail not for me
For death gives me my liberty.

Requiem for the Dead

Upon a dirt and gravel road
I tread to somber music old
The strains of lyrics that shatter souls
Familiar sounds that leave me cold.

I stop as feathered steeds pull hard
To guide their freight into the yard
The breathing of the horses marred
By heavy hoofbeats metal-jarred.

The earth piled high, a hole punched through
Precious cargo, arrives too soon
A dew of tears fall gently down
As soul is committed to the ground.

My heart is shattered, my blood runs cold
Accouterments of the graveyard sold
False promise of eternity
In stone chiseled memory.

And although I turn away from sorrow
It will pursue me through all tomorrows
The churchyard, new home to my beloved
Now serenaded by mourning doves.

The Final Waltz

I've danced with Death
The final waltz
On feet of glass
Faltering, halting
Down white hallways
Towards an unknown light
Leaving broken body
Agony.

I've danced with Death
The final waltz
On winged feet
Ascension bound, Earth unbound
Held safely in ethereal arms
As my soul released
Found joy and peace
Relief.

Colors

Red is life's color
Gray is the color of Death
Blue colors my heart.

Boneyard Voice

Stealth

My heart was broken
When Death, padding on soft paws,
Took you quietly.

Ma Mémoire

When asleep I walk through time
From present to past, further still
I see a fire burning bright
And hear the chime of church bells ringing.

The moans of men, tortured souls
Made sore by glowing firebrands
I see but one in torn and dirty clothes
Now, blackness overtakes me.

Obsidian night and air's cool caress
Awakens me to the horror
Of a woman placed upon the pit
A fire now is kindled.

Her hands are tied behind her back
Hopelessness marks her unlined face
She scans the crowd for one kind look
Burn the Witch! Is their quick response.

Tears flow freely down my face
As I recognize my sister
Not in blood, but energy
In our connection to the Cosmos.

Fire consumes, it spares nothing
On this corporeal plane
My sister's soul flees to the One
And before dawn's break I join her.

Each of the following 26 pages features either a stanza or an illustrative photograph from the series/poem, *The Darker Side of Love*.

The Darker Side of Love

Love is often shown sweet-scented
Bathed in the sentiment of its willing slaves
While just beyond the curtain of poetic license
Lies a darker, clearer truth.

Addiction

Intoxicating love! I pressed you to my breast
You, of the fairer sex, whose eyes gazing into
mine
Brought me to ecstasy unbound, until you left
The high your touch gave me, now replaced with
bottle and needle.

Abuse

You said that I was the center of your universe
Your reason for living
Clinched fists and harsh words prove
earthbound reality
Crimson streaks of blood and black eyes paint
the broader canvas.

Masquerade

Gossamer scarves and handbags
Silk dresses and dinners with friends
All part of the masquerade created to silence
The nothingness, which separates our hearts.

Passionless Love

Kronos forges the river of time
Seconds, minutes, hours gushing, unstoppable
Crushing responsibilities of family and work
Have conspired to rob passion from vows.

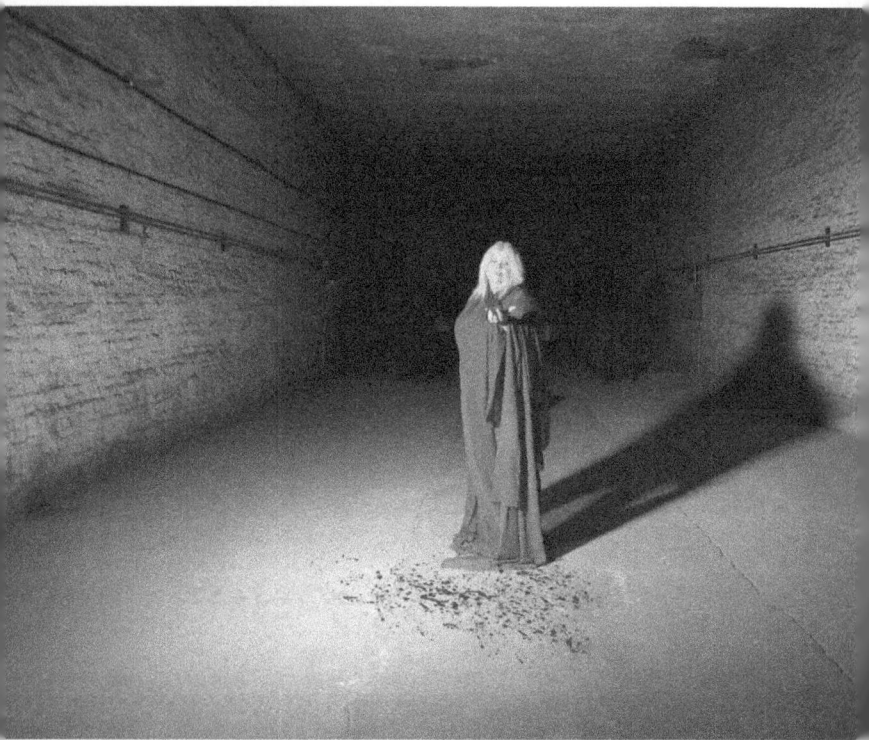

Rage

Emotions ran the color red
Heated words, spoken quickly,
Aimed like artillery to inflict the most injury
To the one you said you'd love forever.

Masks

There was a time when you and I
Would talk about the smallest things, our dreams
I knew you then, before we donned the masks
And lost touch, with each other.

Cold Heart

My heartbeat, hot at the thought of you
Now, banked embers lay where fires once burned
unfettered
Cold mist covers the wreckage of our love
Where black, carrion birds feast.

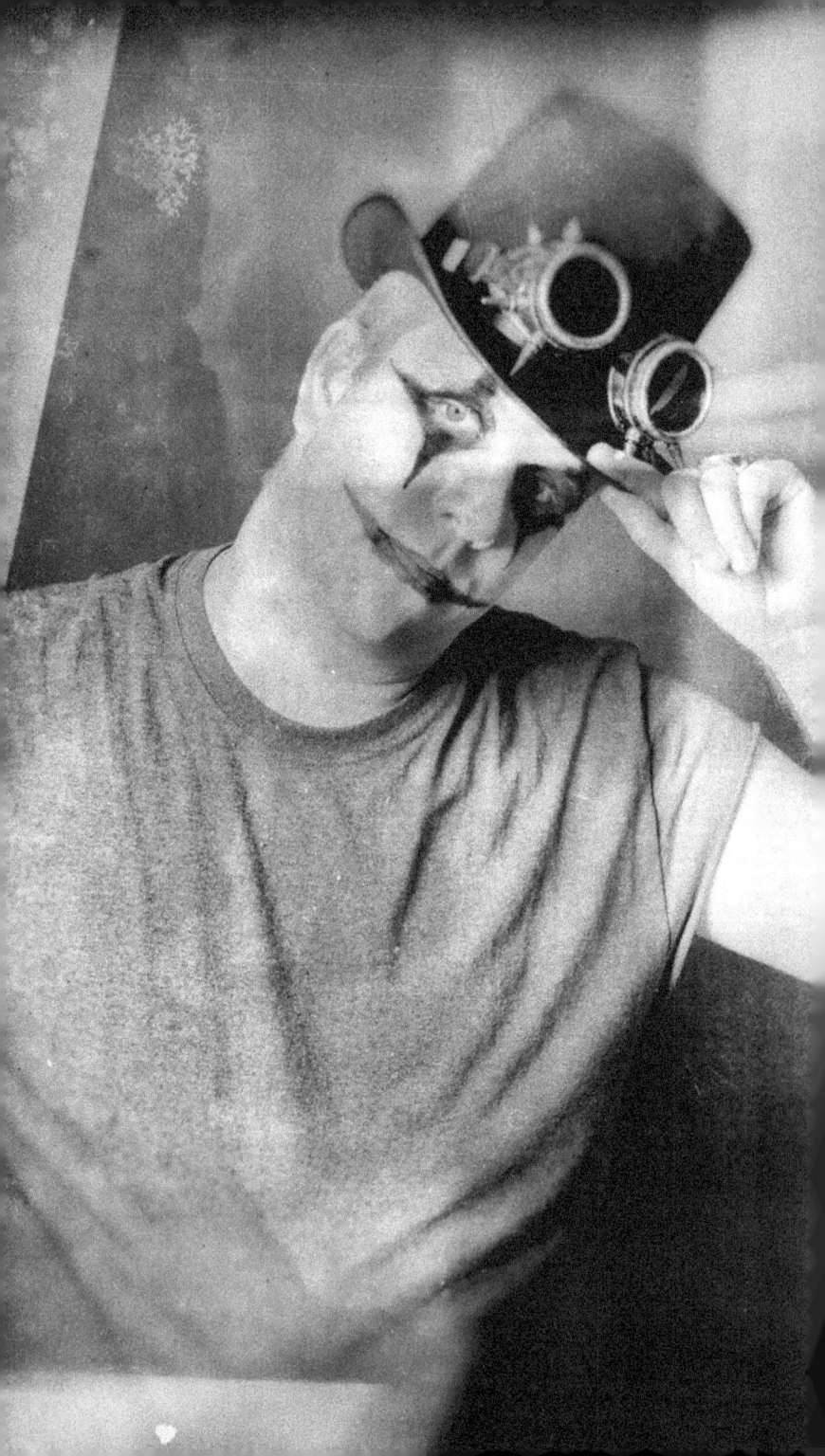

The Ringmaster

I stand in the middle of the ring
A performer of no little talent
Hiding the pain of your indiscretion
Beneath denial and rictus smile.

Shadow Clown

With abandon, I gave up all self-love
To play the clown for you
Dark obsession leads to thoughts of your betrayal
The specter of death begins to sharpen its knife.

Prisoner of Love

My heart condemned to incarceration
For a lifetime and one dark day
In the ravenous shadow of your obsession
My soul starves and withers.

Lost

Waves of eons have flowed through ether
During my search for you
Lifetimes lived on endless seas
Two ships, two captains, two courses.

End of Days

We have danced, the two of us
Through halcyon days lit by golden sunlight
But now, God's dark blue glittering sky
Sets the stage for our final promenade.

Death

Words used like daggers, forgotten
Suspicions of emotions misdirected, forgiven
When the equalizer of souls arrives, fear
While leaving on an ocean of tears, forever.

Missing the Dead

It was a rainy Monday morning,
there was silence all around.

The only noise heard was the pattering of rain
upon the ground.

Out of nowhere a crow flew from a tree.
Oh, what a dark day it turned out to be.

Clouds of gray made up the broad sky.
Broken tombstones lay on top of the hill of those who had
died.

Sorrowful spirits of the bodies in the ground.
Some are angered because their identities were never found.

Families of the deceased still remain hurt,
as corpses and bones lay scattered below the dirt,

Spirits screaming, echoes can be heard far into the night
Souls will awaken to go towards the alluring light.

By Eddie McCowan

Eddie McCowan is a young poet and writer who is drawn to the
darker aspects of life and the inevitability of death. His poetry
reflects the artistic release of his raw feelings and emotions. *Missing
the Dead* was written during a time when he was battling depression
and loneliness. "I felt dead inside. I imagined that my soul was
trapped between life and death. It affected my writing, making it
darker."

Friend him on Facebook at Eddie McCowan.

Credits

The Peaceful Meadow

I sit with closed eyes
As wind, warm from summer sun
Brushes past me, gently kissing face and brow.

The earth beneath my hands
Rich from decay, gives spongy way
As I adjust my position.

My eyes now open
Greeted by absinthe-colored foliage
Marred only by marble obstacles, jarring to the sight.

It is in this place that the dead find peace
And they are most generous in the sharing
Come and sit beside them and me, in this peaceful meadow.

The Peaceful Meadow is dedicated to the multitude of graveyards that I was fortunate enough to photograph over the years, including those featured in some of the images in this book. From the humble cemetery to glorious cities of the dead, these are places of magnificent solitude and reflection. Locations that have in one way or another, served as muses for my dark and unconventional imagination.

As a teenager, I would walk to a graveyard not far from my home, climb a tree, and spend hours reading from my peaceful perch. This dedication is a repayment for those long ago days of childhood when an afternoon in a graveyard would transport me to the otherworld. A place where I still visit, regularly.

71

A special thanks to these locations:

St. Albans Sanatorium
www.stalbans-virginia.com
Radford, Virginia

The Nickerson Snead House
www.thenickersonsneadhouse.wordpress.com
Glade Spring, Virginia

Editors

Heidi Woodruff
Holly Kennedy

www.hauntedphotographer.com
www.pat-okeefe.com
www.patbussard.com

Models

In order of appearance.

Megan Bussard
Cheyenne McGrady
Eddie McCowan
Scarlett McGrady
Adrienne Harless
Jon Matney
Matt Collins
Lilith
Magen King
Stephen Monroe
Nikita Caudill
Jennifer W. Profitt
Ronda Caudill
Holly Mullins
John Edward Ramsey II
Hannah Endsley
Adriona Johnston

Reaper Publishing